Shaped by Our Thoughts

❋❋❋LET OUR PEOPLE THINK❋❋❋

Dr. Murphy V. S. Anderson

DORRANCE
PUBLISHING CO
EST. 1920
PITTSBURGH, PENNSYLVANIA 15238

Dorrance Publishing Co
585 Alpha Drive
Suite 103
Pittsburgh, PA 15238
Visit our website at *www.dorrancebookstore.com*

ISBN: 979-8-89027-012-2
eISBN: 979-8-89027-510-3

"The mind is an essential part of the human body that should not be disposed of unused."

"If you think the mind is too small to comprehend,
store, and process enormous information,
put it to the test."

Table of Contents

Preface

One Friday afternoon about 5:30 p.m., I went for a walk in Sharon Woods' Park. As usual, I go to the park twice or thrice a week for a walk, jog, or to sit by the pond and enjoy nature. The park is one of my three favorite places where I like to hang out and enjoy a quality time by myself, especially when my mind begins to wander into the galaxies of thoughts. For a moment, I was not sure what I was thinking. Perplexed, I soon realized that my mind began to drift deeper into the oceans of memories, quicker into present-day activities, and faster into a utopia. It amazed me to think how wonderful it would be to turn my thoughts of three dispensations (past, present, and future) into a piece of literature for others to read and reflect on. The literature would focus on some of the ills of our time, including ethical, societal, cultural, and traditional issues, and paint a picture of a free, moral, and humane society.

I began writing down my thoughts in my daily journal whenever I was alone. It became clear to me when I found out that each time I visited the park, drove alone in my car, or was in the shower, these thoughts occupied or dropped into my mind. It became imperative for me to write them down immediately for fear of losing them. Each time I was alone in one of these three places, I made sure to have a notepad or a piece of paper and a pen to write down what I was thinking at the time

In this book, I have presented a few thought-provoking reflections on several issues confronting us as a people or society. As a title and subtitle of these reflections, I have selected *Shaped by Our Thoughts* and *Let Our People Think* as found in the Holy Scripture in Proverbs 4:23 (NIV). Though some of these thoughts or "just reasoning" ideas may seem controversial or appear to bridge individual, societal, cultural, or traditional boundaries; this book is not intended to do so. It is not meant to diminish, condemn, or disrespect any individual, group, culture, or tradition.

The content of this book reflects who we have been, what we can be, where we have been historically, and where we might end up, depending on how we treat and appreciate each other and respond to the issues impacting us morally, ethically, mentally, spiritually, culturally, or traditionally. This book is written to encourage all those who believe society can do better than it has already done. It aims to give the reader a self-reflection and motivation to become better citizens of tomorrow.

Each "just reasoning" idea was written by carefully considering specific event(s), individual behaviors, societal issue(s), bridges of culture, and traditional norm(s), which transpired over the past years or are going on currently. For example, a "just reasoning" idea could consider discussions on diversity, racism, justice, or morality as a topic of focus.

Acknowledgments

First, I would like to thank God for giving me the knowledge, inspiration, and courage to compose these reflections. I like to consider myself as a framer of information and someone who is walking the paths of becoming a writer. Often, I wonder how I am inspired with ideas to write, but I am reminded by scriptures that God has given each of us gifts and talents (Ephesians 4:11-16, NIV) that are intended to foster His work, improve our livelihood, and serve each other. Hopefully, it would become evident somedays, that I have a gift of writing.

Second, a special thanks to Mr. Melvin Jones for his collaboration on this book project. Mr. Jones is the artist who designed each portrait used in these reflections. I am grateful to him for his support. Also, thanks to Molly Gottfried for her editing assistance. Her assistance will always be treasured. Lastly, thanks to my kids for their continuous gifts of time and understanding, which have allowed me to focus on my dreams. It would have been difficult to do all that I do without their support.

Dedication

To the impoverished citizens and the memories of innocent lives lost due to domestic carnage.

JUSTICE

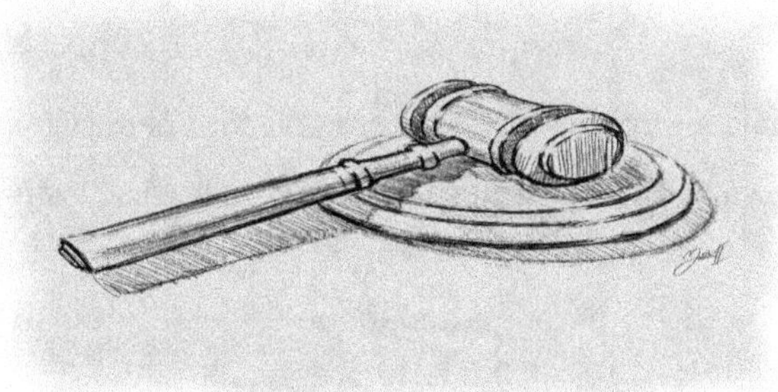

In every courtroom in America and around the world, everyone seeks justice. Everyone deserves justice; whether it is justice for themselves, loved ones, relatives, neighbors, a community member, or a fellow citizen. The fight for justice is historical and imperative. The phrase "let justice prevail" remains perpetual until those who love and desire it lay down their lives to demand and protect it.

From the Nuremberg Trials of Nazi leaders in Germany to the International Criminal Tribunal for the former Yugoslavia President Milosevic, from the Rivonia Trial of Nelson Mandela in the Palace of Justice in Pretoria, to the trial of Charles G. Taylor, by the Special Court in The Hague, from the Ahmaud Arbery murder trial in historic Glynn County Courthouse in Georgia, to the Kyle Rittenhouse trial in Kenosha County Circuit Courthouse in Wisconsin, the cry for justice has become the order of the day. It will remain that way until it prevails over all humankind.

The world searches for justice but never finds her.

Is she too little to be overlooked, too large to be recognized, or invisible to be seen?

Where can justice be found?

Dr. Murphy V. S. Anderson

Who is she that we love her so much?

Where is she that we must find her?

Is she hiding from us or on the loose to nowhere?

We looked on the mountain top, but she was nowhere to be found.

We looked down the valley below and saw her shadow.

We looked to the depths of the oceans, but the waves were too powerful to recognize her.

We looked into the open spaces and heard her cry for help.

We looked in the public arena and heard others discussing her with no respect.

We looked in the courtrooms and found some debating to give her a chance to prevail.

Justice, a seven-letter word, has the authority to change the course of human existence and the power to protect and destroy one's life.

Justice is a friend to no man and an enemy to no system.

She is impartial when her course is defined and upheld by the rule of law.

Justice discriminates against no race or color, sex or gender, nationality, or creed.

She is blind to height, innocent to weight, and favors no statue.

Though she has contenders, she wins every time her name is called in the public square or courtroom.

Justice is not respected of a person, neither is she troubled by their appearance or might.

She is harsh when abused or spoken to disdainfully. She is polite when respected and appreciated.

Justice has no ups or downs, left or right, back or front.

She is impersonal and protects those who seek and honor her.

Justice is invisible but carries the weight of the world on her shoulders.

Shaped by Our Thoughts

Justice speaks no language, holds no citizenship of a country, and is subject to no geographical location.

Justice is practical when moral and ethical people defend her.

She is corrupted when dishonest people set the rules.

Justice is defiant when taken advantage of, accommodating when pursued, protective when acknowledged, and rewarding when obeyed.

We love justice when she's in our favor, hate her when she disciplines us, and resist her when she is against us.

No one knows justice except those who have encountered her.

Justice flourishes when she prevails,

becomes angry when manipulated, and

rebels when denied.

Justice favors no person, social class, culture, or tradition.

She speaks no evil, hears no gossip, and sees no difference.

Justice is never justice until she is justice to all.

RACISM

Racism has been considered by experts one of several reasons for division among Americans. Racism has existed in America for decades and continues to this day. The past waves of racial profiling and degradation in communities and cities across the country has not only resulted in unnecessary deaths of Americans, but it has heightened racial divide and developed a sense of distrust between law enforcement personnel and residents of communities of color. A need to bridge the racial divide and unite all Americans as brothers and sisters cannot be overemphasized and ignored but considered seriously.

Who are you to judge the color of my skin?

Who are you to say that my skin color is not perfect?

Who are you to question the work of the Almighty –

He who made the rainbow in the sky designed me perfectly.

He has made no mistake in designing me.

He loves me like he loves every other race

and designed them uniquely to reflect his creativity and intentions.

God has no regard for color or race; He has made many and cares
about all equally.

Shaped by Our Thoughts

You may not look like me, but we are the same.

Though the color of our skin may be different, we belong to the same Creator and bear His identity.

What has race to do with the blood we share and the air we breathe?

What has race to do with the lives we live?

Is it not God who has given them freely to use?

How much have we paid for the blood we share and the air we breathe?

How much work have we done to enjoy the sunshine and the rainfall?

How much have we paid to walk through the daylight and sleep under the moonlight?

How much sacrifice are we willing to pay to maintain a priceless price for these gifts?

Is there anything we can do to change our race?

Is my race too awkward for you to love me?

Does my race offend you so much to dislike me?

If the color of my skin matters to you, what about the colors of the fish in the sea, birds in the sky, animals in the bush, and creatures beneath the earth?

If my skin color offends you, why did God make your race and other races?

If my skin color annoys you, why do men find pleasure in using them to design cars, houses, clothes, and shoes?

If you hate my skin tone that much, why do you use, wear, or live with things that bear it?

What is the origin of your hate? Who is your maker? Does he live in a different world?

Why are you far from reality? Have you lost your faculty? Have you lost your humanity?

Dr. Murphy V. S. Anderson

Who are your ancestors? Are they from another planet? What has science taught you?

What has your faith and religion helped you to understand about humans?

Did man make you think that your race is superior to others?

Does your maker work in a factory or a manufacturing plant?

Does he know the number of hairs on your head? What elements he used to manufacture your eyes and teeth? Where did he purchase your heart? What instruments did he use to set your body parts in place? Who helped him with constructing you?

Does your maker owe the company where he ordered your parts? Did he rob the banks of different colors to pay his debt? Did he give them a blank check or a promissory note? Does he have enough money to order new parts for you when needed? Is he only here today and gone tomorrow? Where does your maker live?

Look at me! Look at me! I repeat, look at me!

Tell me, what do you see?

Does my anatomy look like yours? Do you have eyes? Do I have eyes?

Do you have ears? Do I have ears? Do you have a mouth? Do I have a mouth?

Where is your heart located? Who put mine in its place? What color is the blood in your veins? Do I bleed water or something else?

All races will die one day and be deposited to the earth, you know!

The earth knows no color and has no respect for the dead. We were made from one dirt and one dirt we shall all return to and unto Him who determined our colors.

Race is insignificant to who we are as humans, you know.

Therefore, love me as I love you.

RAISE EVERY FIST AND STAND

Civil unrest, crimes, violence, demonstrations, and wrongful police engagements with local communities have challenged the last decade. No civil society or governing system can peacefully exist or function amid injustice and inequalities. Therefore, everyone within the society must be treated equally and reasonably to succeed and achieve unity. In the absence of unity and equality, society will demand justice in ways that may not be acceptable.

Raise every fist and stand.

'til hills and valleys hear our faintest cries.

Let our cause on bended knees resound like a roaring sea.

Let every fiber of our being hasten a resolve from above.

God of our ancestors, defender of our solemn cries,

heal our weary hearts.

Bind us together 'til darkness gets no revenge.

Let justice prevail! Let justice prevail!

Let justice prevail 'til every man is set free.

Dr. Murphy V. S. Anderson

Let it warm our hearts and touch our souls

like a dawn of a new day.

Raise every fist and stand.

'til every court, jail, and street corner stand still.

Let every sweat of our brows,

knee to our necks, and bullet to our backs

be lifted 'til justice finds its place.

God of all races, maker of humanity

hear our call, hear our solemn cries.

Let justice prevail! Let justice prevail!

Let justice prevail 'til every man is set free.

Let it warm our hearts and touch our souls

like a dawn of a new day.

God of ages past, God of mankind

unite us with one purpose, one goal, and one destiny.

Soften our stubborn hearts 'til race is considered no more.

Open our mouths to speak the truth,

our eyes to see indifference,

our ears to hear the anguish of the deprived,

our hearts to love each other.

until humanity is set free.

Let justice prevail! Let justice prevail!

Let justice prevail 'til every man is set free.

Let it warm our hearts and touch our souls

like a dawn of a new day.

Almighty fortress, ancient of days,

forget us not; rescue us from injustice,

heal our wounded hearts till they hurt no more.

Omnipotent God; Lion of Judah

uplift our weary spirits to heights of faith and strength

where our enemies may not easily tread.

Let justice prevail! Let justice prevail!

Let justice prevail 'til every man is set free.

Let it warm our hearts and touch our souls

like a dawn of a new day.

ONE MORE DAY

In January 2021, Joseph R. Biden Jr, 46th President of the United States of America, memorialized the lives of 400,000 Americans lost to COVID-19 at the Lincoln Memorial in Washington, DC. On February 22, 2021, the United States reached a staggering milestone of 500,000 deaths due to COVID-19, more significant than the total number of Americans who died in the battles of World War I, World War II, and the Vietnam War combined. This reflection was written assuming what the dead could have wished if they had one more day to live before the COVID-19 took their lives away.

If I had one more day

I would spend more time on bended knees, gaze at the wonders of God and behold his holiness.

I would read my Bible more often and spend quality time with God in prayer and fellowship.

I would enjoy the serenity of the clear blue skies and marvel at the birds as they enjoy the freedom and privilege of God's creation.

Shaped by Our Thoughts

I would lift my nose to the sweet smells of pollen and the blooming
of flowers in the spring.

I would make up my bed in the wind of fresh air and open my ears
to the faintest cries

for justice and peace in our world.

If I had one more day

I would ride on the wings of eagles and soar to heights of humanity
with my ancestors.

I would appreciate life more than I had done or imagined.

I would celebrate my successes and reflect on my failures.

I would appreciate my parents more and thank them for making me
who I have become.

I would spend time and enjoy life with my siblings and dwell in the
comfort of their presence.

I would read more bedtime stories to my kids, create lasting memories, enjoy their company,

and share my life with them.

I would laugh more, smile frequently, resist anger, and love without
borders and limits.

If I had one more day

I would love on my ancestors, spend time with them,

and fest in the abundance of their grace and knowledge.

I would love more, hate less, encourage harder, discourage mean-
ingfully,

motivate impartially and interact more friendly.

I would be more honest in my speech, truthful to my conscience,
obedient to God's will,

faithful to the promises I make, dutiful to the task bestowed on me
by others, and sincere to the relationships I establish with my fellow man.

I would sleep less, work harder, study and learn deeper, think wiser,
and speak fewer.

I would use my knowledge to teach the youth to become better
adults,

exhibit good character to show my elders the lesson they have
taught me,

and bring pride to my community and generation.

If I had one more day

I would ride on the tides of morality & civility and disembark from
the trains of imperfections and divisions.
I would build my dwelling place on the hilltops
and play not in the valleys of wastefulness or uselessness.
I would walk more, sit less, lead majestically, and follow humbly.
I would fear no man but God, defend only my Christian faith,
and believe in nothing else but the Holy Bible.

If I had one more day

I would make God my best friend because his friendship lasts
forever, and I can depend on it.

I AM A HUMAN

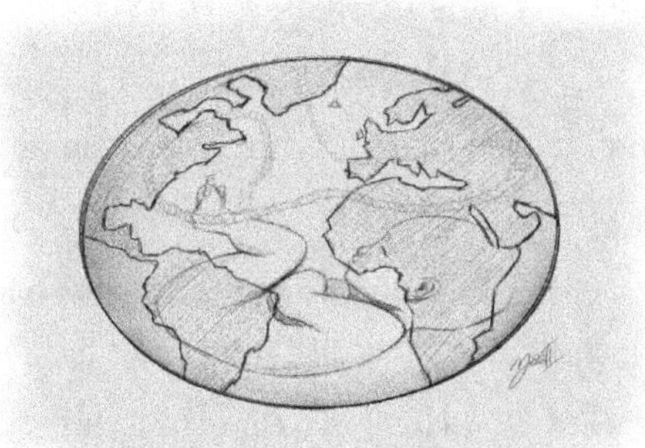

Humans are the only species created in the image and likeness of God. Though there are different races, genders, shapes, heights, and weights, all humans are made from one dust and receive one breath from the same God. Like snow flicks, we are the same, but we are different. Therefore, no race is superior or inferior to the other. We are all humans and God's creation. He loves us all equally, no lesser or bigger than the other.

I am a human, and there is nothing you can do about it.

Please do not hate me but love and appreciate me.

Though my skin may not look like yours, we bleed the same blood and breathe the same air.

Though we look different, our anatomies were fashioned in the image of the same creator, the maker of heaven and earth.

Though you may be richer, wiser, educated, handsome or beautiful than I, we both will die and leave it all behind.

Though you may be buried at Westwood Village Park Memorial and I in a grave of nowhere, the earth knows no color and is not respected of a person.

Though your speech may be eloquent and mine slurred, life and death
are in the power of the tongue.

Though I may be disabled, and you are not, only God knows the
reason why.

Though you may be smiling at me, while I am frowning at you, the se-
crets of our hearts are unknown for the heart is desperately wicked.

I am a human, and there is nothing you can do about it.

Though you may be successful now and I am not, I control my future.

Life may seem better for you and not for me; we share the same
sunshine, rainfalls, night, and day.

Though your name may be called a thousand times and mine never
heard, God knows our names individually. Weeping may endure
throughout my nights, and joy overflows your days;

tomorrow is not promised to us.

I am a human, and there is nothing you can do about it.

Who am I to say that I am better than you and who are you to say
that you are better than me?

Why do we hate each other so much? Why don't we love each other?

Though you may have the power to control or kill me, my soul belongs to God alone.

The tongue and teeth fight, yet they live in the same house. The animals fight for survival but find ways to co-exist peacefully. Nation
revolts against nation, family against family, and sibling against
sibling. After all, they reunite. So why can't we?

Who are you to deny me of my happiness? Who am I to deprive you
of your opportunities?

You are not my maker, and I am not yours.

We were purchased for a priceless price.

We own nothing, desire everything, and must trust nothing but God.

THE ELISABETH - A SYMBOL IN OUR HISTORY

The Elizabeth was one of several ships that sailed the dark waters of the Atlantic Ocean in search of either purchasing slaves or returning freed slaves (settlers) back to the continent of Arica. The Elizabeth, which had a tremendous voyage power was considered the first ship to reach West Africa. On February 6, 1820, the Elizabeth sailed from New York carrying 86 freed slaves (settlers) to Liberia. However, it is believed that there were several other slave ships that bore the name, Elizabeth. The Elizabeth has captured its place in our history and left an indelible imprint on the African slave experience.

For years they looked to the possibility that would set them free
from the shackles of rusty metals, painful incarcerations,
forceful labors, the tyranny of inhumane disposition, and a barrage
of injustice from their masters who held them captive far beyond
the Atlantic Ocean where their boats sailed decades ago.
"Elisabeth," a symbol of our heritage
has captured its place in the history of a nation
where indigenous people born to the land of their forefathers

had exercised their rights to live free and to enjoy happiness.
They were forced into servitude beyond the dark waters
of the Atlantic onto lands
their ancestors had not trodden.
One by one, they lined up in shackles
fastened around their necks and ankles
with few pieces of fabric covering their bodies
from the scorching and blistering burns
of the sub-Sahara sun.
Anger and despair gushingly and copiously
ran down the cheeks of angry but helpless
individuals as they looked in the faces
of those who had come to purchase them
and their fellow compatriots who sold them away.
Cries of anguish burst into the atmosphere
as the captain blew his whistle
and the guards moved in positions.
Feebly and unwillingly, they moved their legs
one step at a time even as the guards yelled,
"Forward march! Forward march! Move it! Move it!"
"Elisabeth," oh how sweet the name sounds
and how majestic our imaginations
transcend this beautiful piece of architecture.
Yet the memories it created in our history
are known and detested by the few who have come to know
the role it played in transporting our ancestors across the Atlantic.
Up towards the boats as they prepared
to sail away on the dark waters of the Atlantic,
a little girl screamed, "Father! Father! Oh, father!
Please do not leave us here by ourselves.
Come back! Come back! Please, come back!
We cannot live without you. Come back, please!"
Faintly and helplessly, she pounded her chest,
buried her tiny feet into the sand along the seashores
as her voice faded away and the warm tears from her eyes

ran down her soft cheeks as though her world had collapsed.

His head dropped as the fading voice

of his little girl began to disappear in the distance

and the boats swiftly sailed away into deep waters.

The shadows of parents, relatives, and loved ones they once lived with

on the land of their forefathers were no more

as darkness engulfed their boats

and images of those left behind slowly

but quietly disappeared in the opened spaces.

"Elisabeth," a dark symbol of our heritage.

Oh, how sweet the name sounds and

how majestic our imaginations transcend

this beautiful piece of architecture.

We will never know the true meaning and

the purpose for its existence unless we know why

it sailed the dark waters of the Atlantic

to the land of our forefathers.

The Love of Liberty Brought Us Here

"The Love of Liberty Brought Us Here" was the founding ideal of enslaved Africans held captive by their enslavers in foreign lands. The attainment of freedom and liberty in their homeland made these enduring and iconic words conceived by formerly enslaved people perfect. These words remain the current motto engraved on the seal of Liberia and a reminder to all Liberians about the untold sufferings and struggles experienced by our forefathers to secure our freedom. We pay homage to them for securing our liberty and freedom.

When the whips lashed, they turned their backs
to their masters to protect their faces.
As the rising sun struck, they sang songs
about their gods and ancestors of ages past.
Hunger raged; they bounded together and fed the weak
with the widow's mite gathered from days worked.
Horses galloped by, and carriages carried their masters.
Barefooted and shirtless tops individuals; they walked to distant areas.
Rain dropped, night fell, and day broke,
yet the dawn of a new day brings no promise of liberty.

Cotton fields and wooden shacks became places of solitude and torture.
Night, a sanctuary of peace, and day, a carnage of distress.
Pitched black darkness buried their identities
as the moonlight exposed their whereabouts.
They bore our pains from the whips on their backs.
They carried our sorrows from the grieves they entrenched in
their hearts.
They secured our future in their fight for freedom and liberty to
find a new home beyond the dark waters of the Atlantic.
The Love of Liberty Brought Us Here!

Oh, how magnificent the inscription of these words in our hearts
that reflect
the hardships and struggles expressed by our fallen countrymen!
How wonderful it is for us to enjoy the liberty given to us by those
who bled and died?
What is liberty without bloodshed, pain, and suffering?
What is liberty without shared values and redemption?
Who guarantees liberty if we do not?
Who advocates for liberty when it is endangered?
Who ensures liberty if we do not protect, know, or appreciate it?
We have survived death at the hands of those who enslaved us,
fought back against those who challenged our freedom.
We defeated the enemies of colonialism, strangled the path of
imperialism.
and ensured the promise of a better tomorrow
The liberty we have and must protect knows no color, creed, tribe,
or religion, but oneness of all humanity.
Let our fight for liberty and freedom be heard deep down in the
graves of justice.
Let it resound to the heights of mountain tops and into the depts of
the oceans.
Let our desire to enjoy it, unify, and bring us together as one nation
and people.

Let our hope to protect and nurture it bears witness to the sacrifices made by those who came before us, those who suffered, bled, and died to secure it.

Lift every heart and stand 'til liberty defeats tribalism, nepotism, bigotry, and sectionalism.

Lift every heart and stand 'til war and division are no more.

Lift every heart and stand until liberty embraces togetherness and brotherhood.

What good is liberty then if liberty is meaningless?

What good is liberty when we do not know its importance?

What good is liberty when we are unwilling to sacrifice and die for her as others have done?

The Love of Liberty Brought Us Here!

The Liberia I Know
A Lamentation

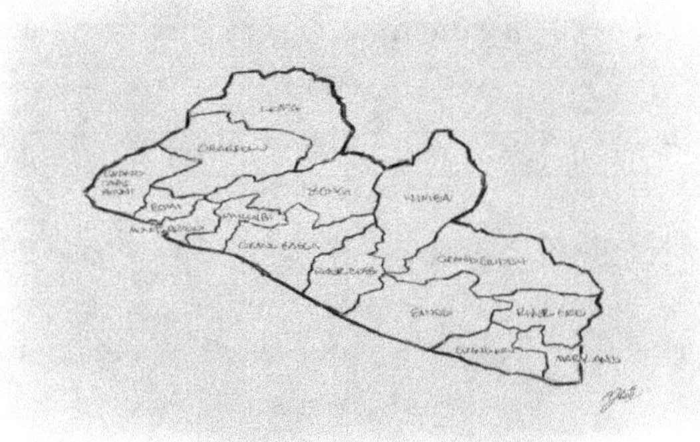

On July 26, 1847, Liberia became the first African and oldest modern republic to declare its independence on the face of the continent. After independence, Liberia became a founding member of several organizations, including the League of Nations, the United Nations, the Organization of African Unity, and the Mano River Union. However, during the last few decades, Liberia has experienced insurmountable challenges, which have driven the nation from its original course of peace, stability, and a "beacon of hope" in Africa.

Liberia, I know today, is not the Liberia I knew as a child who imagined the promises found in these words, "The Love of Liberty Brought Us Here." Liberia today seems to embrace crimes, violence, and mediocrity. It has lost its way into the darkness of unfamiliar paths and headed into the disserts of division, chaos, satanic engagements, and the underdevelopment of human resources. Liberia, I know today seems to tolerate a society of insensitivity, loss of traditional and cultural values, and an overwhelming influence of different ways of life that are negatively impacting our society. Therefore, I lament!

I am *Confused* **by** the compromise of our identity as Liberians
and willingness to settle for anything and everything.
I am *Angry that* we have lost our prominence in the "Community of
African Nations"
and our position as Africa's "beacon of hope."
I am *Frustrated* that we have not learned from our past mistakes,
neither have we learned from other nation's past mistakes.
We continue to engage in the same behaviors and walk the old
paths that led us to the situations we are currently encountering as
a nation.
I am *Terrified* knowing as a people, we are traveling deeper into in-
secure territories,
and there seems to be no concrete plans to redirect our path and
rescue our future.
I am *Worried* that the future of our children and grandchildren is
not promised.
I am worried that we might leave a country worse off and impoverished to our children than we were graciously given by our ancestors and those who came before us.
I am *Frightened* that time is not in our favor; bewildered by the
sluggishness of those in authority to take appropriate actions and
save our nation.
I am *Afraid* that the worst is imminent.
I am *Pessimistic* that our leaders are not concerned about the future of our nation,
and their inactions will further derail the progress already made by
others
to help save our republic.
I am *Embarrassed* that Africa's oldest republic lies in ruins while
other African nations are flourishing and on the brink of socio-
economic developments.
I am *Discouraged* that despite all that we have learned, encountered,
witnessed,
and experienced as a nation, we are willing to do nothing but remain complacent and settle for anything and everything.

However,

I am ***Encouraged*** that all is not yet lost.

I am ***Optimistic*** Liberians are still faithful, willing, and prepared to see a nation rescued, developed, and prosperous for themselves, their children, and grandchildren.

I am ***Hopeful*** that all Liberians will come together, love one another, work with each other to rescue our country from failing and develop it for future generations.

I am ***Prayerful*** that the Almighty God and the blessings of our ancestors will prepare, guide, unite, and lead us as a people and nation to achieving our destiny.

I am ***Determined*** to do my part to rescue and develop Liberia for our children and grandchildren. Are you?

WHY DID WE RUN?

On March 23, 1991, a civil war ravaged the entire West African country of Sierra Leone and resulted in more than 70,000 people dead and left approximately 2.6 million people, more than half the entire population, displaced. A small band of well-armed and funded guerrilla rebels who called themselves "The Revolutionary United Front (RUF)" with the slogan, "Operation No Living Thing," was led by Foday Saybana Sankoh. The civil crisis was by far one of the bloodiest human catastrophes in modern-day Africa.

A Sierra Leonean co-worker of mine informed me about the devastation and untold hardship she, her family, and the families of many others suffered during the crisis. As a Liberian with similar experience and moved by the similarities of our two civil wars, I was challenged to write this reflection.

The oceans were made to serve as a source of food supplies and a means of escape in times of trouble, but they did not do enough to protect us.

God gave us the forests to enjoy nature and as a hiding place from the blazing sun, but they were not wide enough to hide us against the atrocities of man.

Shaped by Our Thoughts

We built homes to shelter our families from the outside, but they were not strong enough to withstand stray bullets and others who came to harm us and destroy our properties.

Therefore, we ran.

The communities were quiet and desolate. Those who controlled the streets looked like us but were not with us.

We feared them; they fear us not!

They held power and authority to take lives or preserve them at will. They were "armies" by day and "gods" by night. We could not resist them but obeyed them. Strayed and targeted bullets flew through the streets from block to block and house to house. They knew no names and had no respect for a person. They were indiscriminately impersonal.

Why did we run?

The bodies of the dead—old, young, mothers, and fathers—lay in the streets as we ran for our lives. Street cats and stray dogs feasted on corpses of those murdered in cold blood or slain by strayed bullets. Cars owned as luxury goods for transportation became immobile and useless to their owners.

We ran to our children; they disowned and abandoned us.

We cried for help from our neighbors; they called us weak and conscripted us.

We ran to bystanders; they could not protect us.

We hid under our beds, but they were too narrow to conceal our identities.

We ran to the rivers and ocean, but the canoes, boats, and ships were already gone.

Our feet were the only means of escape.

Why did we run?

The bullets and guns that were intended to protect us became our enemies.

They were never our friends from the onset. They filled the streets and took residence in the hands of immoral and ruthless thugs who had no regard for human life and dignity.

We had to run because we refused to become dead bodies and be classified as unbearable and uncountable statistics.

We hope to have graves after our days on the earth are over. Our bodies will be in better places if they are buried and returned to their maker rather than be devoured by strayed animals in the streets of nowhere.

Why did we run?

We ran because the babies we gave birth to had become our worst nightmares. We knew them, but they knew us not. They had become children of the unknown and satanic force.

The guns that took the lives of their parents had become their protectors and best friends.

We ran because morality had become a nuisance and evil a public praise. Impartial truth of human dignity and civility had disappeared from the minds of sensible people and replaced by corrupt practices and desires for weapons of warfare.

We ran because we were scared by the unflinching cries of abandoned babies laying in the streets and the anguish of the dead, whose unrecognizable and

decaying corpses were covered by wild flies.

We ran because there were no ups or downs, left or right to run. Animals that once feared us had become the consumers of our murdered parents and relatives.

Why did we run?

We ran because normalcy had lost its place in the shallow graves of evil, deaths, and pandemonium, while friendship and brotherhood were abandoned in the streets of

brutality and bloodshed.

Evil had consumed good as darkness had consumed the daylight. The atrocities committed by night were prevalent and equal to the crimes committed by day.

Respect for human life and dignity had lost its place to national madness and recklessness. Brotherhood and compromise had lost their places to dictatorship and unilateral decision making as the desire, and abuse of arms and heavy weaponry had surpassed the need to co-exist peacefully.

We ran because we could not withstand knowing that a peaceful African nation had lost its prominence in the community of nations.

The Bridge We Must Cross

Since 1847, Liberia has experienced many socio-economic changes and political turmoils. Liberia has experienced several challenges, including military coups, a civil war, tribalism, nepotism, and sectionalism, which have created a national divide amongst tribal and interest groups, political parties, educational establishments, churches, and cultural and traditional societies. Liberia will continue to be plagued by these situations if Liberians fail to correct them. The divide among Liberians will continuously increase unless we put aside our differences, seek a common goal, and cultivate a spirit of nationalism.

When the sun rises,

we must gather out thoughts and

begin the journey across the Bridge.

Like eagles, we must put the wind behind our backs

and soar to heights of faith, knowing that the future is ours to claim.

No, upwards or downwards,

left or right, but forward must remain our fortress.

Shaped by Our Thoughts

We must forge ahead with one mind

one purpose, and one destiny

until our faintest cries are heard beyond

the hallow grounds of our ancestors.

We know our future is secured

because it has been promised.

It awaits us on the other side of the Bridge

because those who came before us worked, bled, and died to ensure it.

With sweat upon our brows,

the sun above our heads,

wind against our chests,

and the strength of our feet,

we must press forward to secure our future.

From the seaport of Harper, Maryland

to the green forest of Gbarpolu;

from the valley terrain of Grand Gedeh

to the steep heights of Mount Wologisi,

and from the grassy mountain range in Nimba County

to the Atlantic Ocean in Montserrado.

The Bridge we must cross may be far

and long, but together

we must focus on the lights ahead

and not the darkness of our past.

We must pick up the weak, weary, destitute

and pull them up to our levels.

We cannot and must not cross the Bridge alone.

Like snowflakes, we are the same, but we are different.

Leaving the weak and weary behind

Dr. Murphy V. S. Anderson

means leaving all of us behind.

Narrow are the roads we walk,

steep the hills we climb, deep the valleys we travel,

and complex the challenges we face, but the Bridge,

we must cross together.

With upbeat spirits and enthusiasm,

renewed mindset, and oneness of purpose,

we must set our gaze beyond the horizon

and envision the land promised to us by our forefathers.

We must climb hand in hand,

back-to-back, with each one of us

pulling the other up to heights

that change our destiny as a people and as a country.

Alone, we benefit not; together we go further.

Yesterday is gone; today is ours to cherish.

The past is the past, and the future we must prepare ourselves.

The Bridge, we must cross together, leaving behind

tribalism, nepotism, sectionalism, war, and hatred.

When "they" come against us, we stick together.

When we go against "them," we go together.

We cannot cross the Bridge unless we see it together.

We cannot see it together unless we know it.

We cannot know it

unless we are willing to learn about it.

We cannot learn about it

unless we are willing and prepared to learn about it together.

THE CONFUSED CITIZEN

He was born into a family of Zoes (Zows – Lorma) and would eventually become a tribal leader to succeed his ancestors when he reached adulthood. In his local vernacular, his name, Tanue (Lorma) means an owner of a town or village. They called him Zowoi Tanue because of his inheritance and future traditional role he would have assumed in his local village. The elders and societal elites (Zows) recognized his distinct personality and traditional leadership qualities upon birth and moved to name him. They knew that he would some days succeed them as chief zow upon their demises. However, his parents were not sure who he was or would eventually become.

He struggled to live in two worlds, life as a traditionalist and a city dweller. He decided that he would live a life contrary to the meaning and responsibilities of his traditional name and would not conform to upholding and protecting his traditional values and cultural practices. He surprised his parents, elders, and other members of his village when he informed them, he was leaving for the city. He wanted a life in the West beyond the Atlantic and not in Africa. "Living abroad makes me a man than becoming a traditional leader," he stated.

Dr. Murphy V. S. Anderson

Haven't you seen that man?

Haven't you heard what he has to say about himself?

Where is he from, and where has he gone?

Doesn't he look strange?

Do you know the man?

"Yes, I do!" one passerby said!

"No, I do not," another bystander exclaimed.

From the arena, the words echoed,

"Who are you, and where are you from?"

"I am a citizen, a born citizen!"

"I need not tell you where I am from.

I am a citizen."

"No, you're not!"

A resounding voice echoed

from the far-right side of the arena.

"You're confused!"

"Indeed, you're confused!"

The voice added.

"We have confused him!"

"We have betrayed him!" one voice said.

"How have we confused and betrayed him?"

Another voice asked.

"We did not teach him well!"

"We have failed him and left him to his faculty."

Sometimes, he knows where he is from, but

he is confused about his origin at other times.

When asked on the radio,

Shaped by Our Thoughts

he says, "I am a citizen, a born citizen!"

When asked by one of his own,

he says, "I am a naturalized citizen."

Who is this confused citizen?

Has he lost his mind?

He dresses against his cultural values

to impress others or

fit in with those he considers his kind.

He changes his tone of voice

to sound like someone else, but he is not.

He knows not to wear the fabric of his ancestors

in the public arenas to avoid exposure to his identity.

He braids his hair like a female

and wears dreadlocks to look cute and attract attention.

He uses his body like canvas or

street walls to paint graffiti,

images of people, things, and words he adores.

He is in denial of himself

and misrepresents his cultural values and norms.

He is angry with his race and sex.

He accuses his maker of making a mistake in creating him.

He defies the existence of God

as though he was never taught who God is

and what he has done for him.

He forgets the promises he made to God

in the heat of the moment.

He accuses his creator in the court of public opinion

for creating him a "Black man."

Dr. Murphy V. S. Anderson

He gnashes his teeth and tightens his fist

as he walks through the auditorium of historical personalities

and sees a picture of another Black man

hanging on the walls.

He is spiteful! He is self-condemning!

He uses profanity like inmates

in state prisons and has no regard for his elders.

He sticks his head above his shoulders

as though he is a god or a bigot.

He spends money lavishly

as though he has no past to remember, present

to be concerned about, or a future to consider.

He is alone and has no wife or children.

He has no regard for his mother.

He tells her the food she cooks is foreign

and smells like skunk.

He treats his father like his enemy

and disgraces him in the public square.

Who is this man?

We must ask ourselves.

His ancestors look down

from the heavens and are upset with him

because he has gone astray, but he cares less.

He is a confused citizen!

He looks at society disdainfully

and has no remorse for his disrespectful conduct

against his fellow citizens.

History has taught him no lessons

Shaped by Our Thoughts

neither has his questionable faith

taught him morality or spiritual values.

He fearlessly and disrespectfully engages others –

the weak, poor, elderly, and his peers –

as though he has no moral compass.

His farfetched ambitions and unrealistic dreams

are unachievable.

They have forced him to change his sexual orientation

and driven him deep down into the dungeons of

drug addiction, the oceans of crimes,

and dark pathways of illegal practices,

which have led him into mental imprisonment,

social isolation, economic deprivation, and financial hardship.

He cannot afford the food he eats,

a place to stay, or the clothes he wears on his back.

He depends on others to take care of him,

yet, he is arrogant and acts like "all that" or owns the universe.

We know him because we made him

and brought him onto this platform.

He knows us not and is careless about who we are!

He is a confused citizen and knows not

his ancestors or country of origin.

All he knows and cares about

are those he surrounds himself with

and the country he finds himself within.

He is lost, totally lost!

He is bemused about his existence

and perplexed about his identity.

Dr. Murphy V. S. Anderson

He refuses to be one of us

or be identified with us.

Who is this man?

We have sold him to another nation

by our failure to teach him our culture and traditions.

We have enslaved him to different ideologies

by our deliberate and perpetual refusals

to impact him with our spiritual and moral beliefs.

We have exposed him to a new way of life

that is inconsistent with ours and

have abandoned him in the streets

of thugs and prostitutes.

He is high on drugs and speaks slurred

as though he has found a new language.

He brags about his association with the wrong crowd

and beats his chest violently, claiming,

"I am the man" "I am the man"

When he addresses his siblings.

His parents are afraid of him

and so are his siblings and relatives.

But they have no choice

but to love him and own him.

He hates society and is against anyone

who tries to make him a good citizen.

He prefers death than being alive.

He believes death has become a nuisance

and living a chance that one must contemplate daily.

He equates success to materialism

Shaped by Our Thoughts

and struggles to an individual's laziness

and failure to strive harder.

He views religion as man's organization

of poor people who have no basic premise in life

but enjoy congregating and having fun.

He believes Christians are weak-minded individuals

and baggers who constantly disturb the "god"

they trust and worship by calling on his name repeatedly.

He is far from reality and has no self-identity,

determination, or awareness.

He claims to know it all

and considers everyone beneath him.

He is arrogant, self-destroying, and deceitful.

His poor mannerism is driving his neighbors

and friends into social distance and

has left him lonely and isolated.

He needs help, but fails to recognize

his inabilities to become self-reliant.

We must help him quick

or else lose him.

Who is this confused citizen?

Has he gone too far into the wilderness of life?

Have we lost him?

Do we have time to rescue him?

Where can we find him?

We must ask ourselves to find the answers.

THE POWER OF GOD

What is a power that man loves so much? Who is man that he has no regard for the essence of power? Why has man become consumed by power? Who gives him power that he has become so drunk with it and seems not to understand how to use it? From the beginning of creation 'till now, God's power has been manifested throughout the existence of humankind. His majestic power cannot be compared or measured to any other powers. God is the highest power; he is bigger and greater than all other powers in the universe and the heavens.

As a kid, I did not know who controls the power of existence.

I have driven an automobile at the fastest speed that my hands could control.

I have flown in a plane and marveled at the magnificent power of two tiny engines thrusting a

fast-moving object into the sky and maintaining it in midair.

I have a massive ship ply a might ocean and it never sinks.

I have seen the sunrise, the rain fall, felt the wind blow, and the
breeze stand still.

I have seen darkness wrestle with light for control, and night dis-
engage day as the earth rotates.

I have read about the rising of nations and the falling of some.

I have read about Adolf Hitler and Mussolini conquering the world,

but eventually they lost power and died.

I have experienced the sufferings of humanity and witnessed their
prosperity.

I have seen the birth of a baby and his death in one lifetime.

I have seen the changes of the seasons and gazed at the splendid
handiwork of God in the sky.

I have seen the power of one man's talent entertain his fellow men
as others weep tears of joy.

I have seen flowers bloom and fade away.

I have seen a man who served God with his life but dies and leaves
the world behind.

I have heard predictions about the end of the world but did not
come to pass.

I have listened to the preaching of hundreds of sermons and have
realized that the power to be saved rests in the word of God and not
the preacher.

I have seen the rising tides, the waves of the ocean, and the falling
of the same.

I have seen the mighty power of tornadoes and heat waves, tsuna-
mis, and earthquakes.

I have seen life without purpose become purposeful, a murderer
become God-fearing,

and a drug addict cleaned.

I have seen one man beat up his opponent in the ring for money
and die leaving it all behind.

I have seen the ascension of man to the moon and his failure to reach the heavens.

Now that I am older, I have not seen power so perfect, resoundingly majestic, and unequivocally uncontested than the Power of God.

Who is like unto thee, for your power is everlasting?

Just Thinking Moments
Past, Present, and Future

"I do not focus on my past because that was yesterday; what happened yesterday may not be the same today. I reflect on my past because it taught me unforgettable lessons, but it is gone now. I celebrate my present because it lives with me in this moment. Whatever I do now will determine my tomorrow. I celebrate my future because I have not done much yet. My future is yet to come! I look to my future because it gives me hope to live on and provides endless opportunities for me to do great things. Whatever I plan to do in my future, I do with respect for the lessons learned from my past, humility for my present and deep sense of appreciation and awakening for the future."

Arrogance

"Arrogance and stupidity win when wisdom and knowledge flee the arena of life."

Stupidity

"Stupidity will prevail when wisdom and knowledge are suppressed by wise men."

Evil

"Evil transcends good when the moral compass of humanity is entrusted in the hands of wicked and lawless leaders."

Creativity

"Necessity and Opportunity result to Creativity. Creativity never occurs in the absence of necessity and opportunity."

Perception

"Perception is the mirror in the back of our minds that forces us to accept or reject things the way we think based on our personal convictions."

Preparation

"Preparing early avoids unnecessary mistakes; preparing on time is an invitation to making avoidable mistakes."

Spirituality

"A compromise with one's spirituality is a death sentence to one's eternity."

Aging

"Aging is not a choice; it is an inevitable phenomenon of life that is **only** avoided by death."

Courage

"The sun that shines **MUST** first rise."

Education

"Education allows us to exhibit our humility, but arrogance forces us to demonstrate our stupidity."

Hard Times

"When Joseph becomes the leader in your palace, your pharaoh will flee."

Problems

"The reason why we do not think much about yesterday is because today has a lot to consider and tomorrow much more to worry about."

"Why think about tomorrow when you have not solved today's problems or resolved the problems of yesterday? Tomorrow has its own problems. Remembering the problems of yesterday and resolving today's problems will better prepare you for tomorrow's challenges."

The Future

"The future belongs to one person; the one who thinks about it and prepares for it."

Character

"If you do not stand for something, you will fall for everything and end up getting nothing or doing anything."

Evil

"The evils that are perfected in our world today were not first birth in industrial facilities, manufactured in scientific laboratories, planted in fields of agriculture, or created in the walls of academic institutions; they were conceived on the platform of Man's mind as was initially masterminded by his ancestors against the Creator. Man has chosen to perfect these evils even though history proves that evil is senseless, wicked, and has no reason to exist."

Knowledge

"Do not die knowing NOT what you should have known or done to make life worth living for you and your fellow human being."

Success

"Success is a direct result of thoughtfulness, determination, and preparation."

Longevity

"Longevity is not a determination for superiority but an expectation of good performance."

Life

"Life is a motion; it moves wherever it pleases."

Writing

"Writing is like walking down a road. You must look on all sides of the streets to capture movements of things, objects, and people to guide you during your thinking and writing process."

Notes

Allo, A.K., (2020). The courtroom as a site of epistemic resistance. Mandela at Rivonia. *Law, Culture, and The Humanities Journal, 16*(1) 127-150. https://doi.org/10.1177%2F1743872116643274

Bekiempis, V. (2021, January 19). Joe Biden holds memorial for 400,000 Americans who have died of Covid-19. *The Guardian.* https://www.theguardian.com/world/2021/jan/19/biden-coronavirus-memorial-us-deaths-ceremony

Bible Gateway. (n.d.). *Ephesians 4:11-16.* https://www.biblegateway.com/passage/?search=Ephesians%204%3A11- 16&version=KJV

Gasser, G., & Quitterer, J (2015). The power of God and miracles. *European Journal for Philosophy of Religion, 7*(3). https://doi.org/10.24204/ejpr.v7i3.114

Grosscup, S. (2004). The trial of Slobodan Milosevic: The demise of head of state immunity and specter of victor's justice. *Denver Journal of I ternational Law and Policy, 32*(2). https://digitalcommons.du.edu/djilp/vol32/iss2/7/

Hodge, C. C., & Nolan, C. J. (Eds.). (2007). *U.S. presidents & foreign policy. From 1789 to the present* (p. 49). ABC-CLIO.

Hutchinson, B. (2021, October 17). Ahmaud Arbery murder case may evoke Georgia's history on race: Experts. ABC News. https://abcnews.go.com/US/ahmaud-arbery-murder-case-evoke-georgias-history-race/story?id=80522209

Jalloh, C. C., (2015). The law and politics of the Charles Taylor case. *Denver Journal of International Law & Policy, 43*(3). https://ecollections.law.fiu.edu/faculty_publications/248/

Kaldor, M., & Vincent, J. (2006). *Case study Sierra Leone. Evaluation of UNDP assistance to conflict-affected countries.* United Nations Development Programme Evaluation Office. http://web.undp.org/evaluation/evaluations/documents/thematic/conflict/SierraLeone.pdf

Lambert, C. (2018). "The love of liberty brought us here": Writing American identity in Liberia, 1830-1850. *Irish Journal of American Studies, 7,* 3–12. https://www.jstor.org/stable/26489188

Smith, D. (2021, November 19). *Watch now: Jury finds Kyle Rittenhouse not guilty in Kenosha shootings.* Kenosha News.https://www.kenoshanews.com/news/local/watch-now-jury-finds-kyle-rittenhouse-not-guilty-in-kenosha/shootings-article_571bd314-09ff-567b-b1f9-0e60c1d09334.html

Sinclair, D. (1924, May). The power of God. *Christian Science Journal.* https://journal.christianscience.com/shared/view/1t31s2uv3n4

Tomuschat, C. (2006). The legacy of Nuremberg. *Journal of International Criminal Justice,* 4(4), 830–844. https://doi.org/10.1093/jicj/mql051